The Must Have, Do-This-Then-That, Direct Mail Marketing Checklist
For Every Real Estate Entrepreneur

The Secret To Seller Marketing That Most Investors Will Never Know About...And You Hope Your Competition Never Discovers

How To Discover Your Target Market (Faster), Reveal The Selfish Desired Results They Want (Easier) and How To Make Sure You Are The One They Buy From (Automatically)

A Free Report
By Erik Stark
www.TheRealErikStark.com
www.EriksFreeBook.com

The Secret To Seller Marketing Most Investors Will Never Know About…And Your Competition Hopes You Never Discover

Copyright © 2018 Erik Stark
Printed in The United States of America
ISBN 978-0-359-09769-2

Erik Stark
Erik@TheRealErikStark.com

You may download your digital copy of this report at
https://TheRealErikStark.com/sellermarketing
for additional resources and live links.

Download Your KPI Worksheets Here.
TheRealErikStark.com/KPI

Before you press play on your next marketing campaign, take the time to sit down and run through this checklist of proven questions that will help you zone in on some key factors that determine the QUALITY of leads you receive.

By taking the time to implement these variables you will operate your marketing with clearer focus (due to absolute clarity of knowing WHO you are attracting), less frustration (since your marketing will explain your services instead of you always being that message) and measurable progress along the way (because you will have segmented your marketing with so much focus you can easily determine which messages and campaigns are giving you the best return).

This is just the very beginning of a very deep rabbit hole, however, if you implement these strategies you will have a strategic advantage over your competition because you are choosing to educate your audience, not badger them.

Thank you for choosing to invest in yourself. What you are about to reveal was one of the monumental shifts in our real estate business that repositioned our value in the marketplace that resulted in less deals with higher pay days, less resistance and more harmonic transactions, less distraction and more clarity...all with measurable statistics that we could tweak and improve along the way.

We're in this together. For you, we are grateful.

Selecting Your (Hyper Focused) Target Market...

I am excited to jump right in and share what the worlds greatest companies do to become giants in their industry. Few, if any real estate companies creating marketing that serves their industry. By implementing this, you will gain a strategic competitive advantage over your competition and improve your market share in your local industry.

When you can speak to someone with direct, intentional focus, you move the dynamic of that relationship into a level of trust by allowing them to recognize that you understand a need they have. No one cares how much you know, until they know how much you care.

Magnetic marketing _begins_ when you begin to speak to your prospects (regardless of how large that list may be) with direct, intentional focus.

It compounds when you solve their need with that intentional focus.

It comes full circle over time as they repeatedly come back to you for additional information and before you know it, the client who only came for information, is now coming for business.

In order to do this, you have to know **who** SPECIFICALLY you are searching for. This process can be tough because the human brain thinks you are abandoning ALL the target markets in search of just one.

However, savvy businesses know that there are riches in niches.

Take for example the household goods industry.

When you have a toothache and walk down the aisle for toothache medicine, does it ever occur to you that EVERY one of those boxes or tubes is owned by 1 of 4 companies?

Of course it doesn't.

Those same companies also specialize in headache medicine, arthritis, pain relief, stomach relief, fungus relief, baking soda, laundry detergent and a host of other relief aides and household goods that allow you to obtain some result RIGHT NOW.

These companies have done an incredible job segmenting their products down to the ridiculous to make sure somehow, some-way, their product meets the need of that specific market. If ever you get caught up in the overwhelm of this process, simply look to industry giants like Johnson & Johnson, Proctor & Gamble or Arm and Hammer.

Im willing to bet not 1 of the executives lives with the belief that they are _**just**_ a "house hold goods and relief aid company"

So what does this mean to the "we buy houses" guys whose only care is to buy real estate?

Well, it could mean a change in the right direction if you begin looking at your business as a solution center for consumers who have multiple different needs.

Think about it. You "just" buy houses.

Yet behind every single one of those deals was some unique story, problem and solution that had to be overcome in order to "just" buy another house.

Problems and solutions that make you an expert.

An expert who speaks a certain language and who has a specialized set of skills.

Language and skills that once identified and communicated to properly would allow you to segment that language into a message that attracts customers *who only want those results*.

Think of the moment when product developers learned Arm and Hammer served multiple uses. Do you think they just went around introducing this miracle powder?

It became a stain fighter. Teeth whitener. Odor reducer. Pool treatment. Skin exfoliator. Carpet cleaner. Allergy reducer. Volcano reactor and literally hundreds of other uses.

Do you think if we left it up to ourselves to learn all of what this miracle powder can do for us that it would be the name it carries today?

So why then would we just remain a "we buy houses" company?

At this point you may realize that there are several "ideal" target markets inside of your target market. Focus on those that are "hyper focus targeted", most likely to do business with you and offer you the largest payday opportunity for the relief you provide.

This is the same reason laundry detergent companies offer multiple choices in their products. Some people just want the whitest whites. Some want the smell of lavender. Some want something that is easy on colors. While some just want pure cost effectiveness.

What you will find amongst the majority of these products is that the base of their functionality gives the exact same result.

It's simply communicated to people differently which allows them to identify more market share and pull them from another brand into their world.

So think about your ability to buy houses and how easy it is for us to just pay cash and close the deal. Thats the easy part.

However when you factor those on the other side of the fence, they have a whole world of items that need to be resolved before they can just accept your cash and move on.

Some have code violations to deal with. Some need to evict tenants. Some need to settle probate. Some need to resolve title issues.

Everyone brings something different forward that gives us an opportunity to provide an up front solution and earn their business for life...or at least the life of the transaction.

The solutions you provide are _ultra specific_ to the niche you serve. Therefore the questions you ask to help determine how you will attract clients who need these service's must be well thought out and provide up front value.

Here are some questions to consider asking and answering that will help you identify your greatest opportunities in a given target market.

Who do I serve BEST in my business?

Who frequently tells me that they are grateful for the help I provided them?

Who am I known as in the local market?

Out of all my transactions, what is the common lead source or common thread of deals I do the most of?

Who do I find myself marketing to the most?

What sort of deals do I do the most of?

In my experience, the fastest way to determine your most profitable target market is to look at the past 1 years transaction history and determine the lead source for every transaction.

These are known as your KPI's

If you did 15 deals, and out of those 15 deals, 10 were probates, 3 were short sales and two were referrals, Id bet to say that you have a strong language and skill for consistently closing probate deals.

You are an industry expert on probates.

Somewhere in your language you possess the ability to give someone a speedy result when it comes to probates.

Use this process to determine your ideal target market and Ill show you how to discover those who want what you specialize in.

If you are not absolutely clear on WHO you are wanting to attract with your magnetic marketing, you will actually repel them by just being another marketer saying "look at me, Im better than the next guy" rather than educating them and solving a problem for them NOW that keeps them coming to you for more information.

I want you to use the medicine industry as a good base line for determining if you are positioning yourself properly. Always revert to the pros of an industry as the standard you are working towards.

Notice how you never feel "pitched" to and their messages just seem to be at the right place at the right time.

So lets begin to select your first hyper focused target market. Don't worry about trying to capture all of them. We begin with your first, most profitable lead source and then simply take the language you speak and the relief you provide and make it available through non invasive, indirect response mechanisms that provide relief to your market.

Do you know which target market you are starting with?

If not, use the KPI strategy to go over your last 1 year of transactions and break down…

1. How many deals did you do in the last year
2. The source of each deal
3. The overall profit on each deal
4. How do you rate that deal on a scale of 1-10?
5. The average profit of each lead source

Your average profit will be the tell all of your most profitable deal sources. Once you figure it out, use this as your ideal target market to begin with.

Once you do know your first target market you are beginning with, its time to move on to determining how you will solve their problems and just exactly how will you begin to get these clients to step forward and request your information.

SIDE NOTE* If you can treat this process as if you are speaking to one person, you will impact far more than if you try to apply this to everyone.

What Form Of Media Will I Use To Capture Their Attention?

This is such a vital piece of your successful marketing. We see many investors who are looking for long time landlords (who are generally over 50 years old) and spending all of their money trying to find these sellers on Facebook.

Another horrible example is the US Post Offices Every Door Direct Mail program. I recall having a conversation with one of the market reps letting him know I was looking for landlords in a specific zip code. His genius idea was for me to send a postcard to EVERYONE in that zip code.

I casually explained to him that this was a poor way to capture landlords because the simple fact that I was banking on the only landlords that would receive my message, were those who lived in the same zip code where I was trying to buy these properties.

I know from experience that a landlord who lives across the county, across the state and certainly across the country will be far more likely to sell than one who lives 4 streets over.

This rep told me that the tenants could also forward my mailer.

The bottom line was it was simply absurd what this guy said. He insisted that he had several Realtors who used this successfully, and maybe so, however not using it the way I intended.

However this is what you are going to get if you just "go with the flow" and do what the masses say to do. You"ll have to abandon this mass thinking and begin to observe what truly successful companies do and then do some additional out of the box thinking.

You have to know the demographics of your target market and where they go for information.

Designing your media around the answers to these questions will allow you to not only see your product or service from your clients perspective, but by answering these honestly, you have already done most of the copywriting and leg work of structuring your words to compel your customer to take action.

Obviously you can choose between direct mail, news paper ads, advertorial style marketing, Facebook, online lead generation, etc. However if you're searching for old landlords like my grandma who owns quite a few investment properties, you are much better off getting her attention by putting your advertisement on the local diners placemat instead of getting her to respond to a postcard.

Not only is this her era, but she has a biased opinion towards shiny, bright colored mailers promising her the moon and then not delivering. She doesn't trust direct mail so therefore my message gets ignored.

There is no absolute right or wrong answer however by deeply understanding WHERE your target market is looking for solutions, you can largely influence the success of this process.

Here are some key questions to consider before creating your magnetic marketing.

Where is my target market looking for answers?

What questions are they asking to discover these answers?

How are they seeking results for their questions?

Why would they act or not act?

What can I give them NOW that will allow them to discover my services?

Answers these question IN DEPTH and at a core level. The deeper you dig in revealing the pain points of your clients, the more likely they are to respond and view your offer as valuable information.

This IS the secret behind creating magnetic marketing.

If your answers are surface level, then your responses will be mediocre.

Notice how you don't receive direct mail notices for creams and medicines. They strategically put those in mens health magazines, golf, women's health, pediatrics and in areas where people frequently need those sort of results.

The reason these questions are important to consider now is because you are going to weave these into your media forms to help identify customers who are interested in what you specialize in.

Here are some ideas of media forms and how people can raise their hand to begin communicating with you…

• Oversized Mail Media
• Pre Recorded Messages
• SIMPLE Websites with Your Specific, Direct Message (NO INFO OVERLOAD) and How To Receive it
• Self Address Stamped Envelopes (Remember These?)
• Web Video
• Free Book (<——My personal favorite)
• DVD Request
• Media USB Stick
• Personalized URL
• Press Release
• Testimonial Video
• Resource Guide
• Free Report
• FAQ Forum
• Live Call In For Questions and Answers
• Facebook Groups

What Is My Compelling, Mafia Style Offer?

These questions are the foundational baseline for all marketing you create for each of your target markets.

People are naturally selfish, so if you expect them to respond to WE BUY HOUSES in 3 DAYS, then you will be continuously disturbed as more of this type of marketing becomes saturated in our industry. There needs to be a clearly identifiable *SPECIFIC* benefit to them doing business with you.

When you make the dynamic shift to educate your market on a **relevant** pain point they are dealing with, such as a nasty eviction, then the we buy houses becomes a **result** of the value that you are providing to them, usually in the form of relief.

Remember, they are not looking for We Buy Houses guys or a real estate agent. They are looking for relief for their tenant problems.

I asked my wealthiest real estate mentor how he was able to buy so much real estate in such a prime area of South Florida.

His answer was profound, "I sought out the largest property owners in town and offered to buy their property. If they said no, I offered to manage it with more guaranteed profitability and for 2% less than the competition or even for free if they gave me the first right of refusal to purchase when they decided to sell".

This is pure genius for the fact that he created an offer that few landlords will refuse. They get increased income, decreased expenses with no downside other than giving him the first choice to pay more than the current offer they receive when they took it to the market.

My mentor knew that by getting to know the ins and outs of a properties performance he could move ultra quick with deciding. He also knew that as the relationship grew with those he was managing, it became easier for them to just "get down to business" when they wanted to sell.

This is why he is one of the single largest independent landlords who is worth just under $2,000,000,000 (yes 2 billion).

Step into your ideal target markets shoes. What could you provide to their problem **right now** and give such a strong appeal to it that there is no way for them not to consider taking the offer?

Think of how you communicate in real life. You don't offer your closest relationships "generalized" information when they are going through something tragic or tough. You take the time to get specific and offer valuable information that will relieve them of the overwhelm now.

While mastering this is form of communication requires some additional thinking, the rewards are immense as you scale your business and slowly pull ahead of your competition with directional intent and measurable progress.

TheRealErikStark.com/SellerMarketing

What problems are they currently having that I can solve for them right now?

What is the conversation they are having in their head about this problem?

What is the compounding effect of not solving this problem?

Where are they searching for answers to these problems?

Who else is also providing solutions to these problems?

What would prevent them from acting on something that would solve this problem?

What can I offer them as an incentive to respond?

How do I present this offer to look like valuable info instead of an ad?

What is their perfect result I can deliver them?

What would make my perfect client raise their hand to receive more information?

My personal favorite is, **WHY, with all options available to them, including doing nothing, should this person choose to do business with you?**

By creating these in depth answers and thinking like your customer, you learn what "Triggers" they may respond to that would allow you to create A direct response, highly valuable offer.

The offer allows you the ability to give them an immediate result based on the trigger they responded to. When you meet these selfish desires of human nature, its natural to want to receive more.

What is your "to good to say no" offer that will allow people to step forward and into your world where you can begin engaging and continue to provide value to them?

Does My Marketing Make It Easy To Respond?

A perfect example of what I see frequently are bandit signs that direct someone to visit a website. When someone is driving, the best option would be to call a phone number or text-to-receive.

The likelihood of someone driving by your sign, running errands and then going home to visit your website is very minimal.

Make it easy to respond.

The goal is to give them a solution they can act on RIGHT NOW.

Make it easy for them to respond like a pre recorded message where they can leave their contact information and have you mail a report out to them.

Or include a self addressed, stamped envelope and make it easy for them to send back the request for more information.

People are lazy (I speak for myself actually) and if they have to jump through hoops to receive your information, unless you are offering free money, they will likely skip over your request.

I know I do.

TheRealErikStark.com/SellerMarketing

Answer these questions and answer them again to get to the core about how you can truly make it easy for people to do business with you.

How will my prospect most willingly respond to my ability to help?

How can I get them to take action now?

What possible barriers would prevent them from taking action?

Can I deliver an immediate solution upon their first contact with me?

How can I repurpose my response to cover multiple different ways of responding?

Giving them the option to wait until later to take action will kill your response rates. Direct response means taking action right this moment.

Give them the ability to do so.

The reason this works so amazingly well with toothache medicine is cause they have the market cornered and if you need a result, you're only going with 1 of 4 options.

Although they love a "right now" sale, they realize that if you walk out Targets door cause the price was too high, they are still going to capture your sale over at Walmart or Walgreens.

If you have a headache, there are not all that many options and they realize if you want immediate relief, they have made it as easy as it possibly can be.

Today offers a plethora of ways to respond and when you pair this together with multiple different options, you will be carving out your portion of the marketplace and over time, own more and more market share.

Some of the best options for pairing these response mechanisms with a non invasive process are…

Optin through FB login and follow up through messenger.

Newspaper advertorials with pre recorded message responses.

Dine in placemats with text to response information.

Offer for free report and follow up via email or text.

Free incentive in exchange for Facebook like.

Visit website for a self market analysis (no human contact).

Resource guide

Even offering a One Touch Facebook login will help to improve response rates vs requesting email.

How Am I Capturing Their Info To Continue Giving Them Valuable Information?

In the digital marketing world, most people consider this an "opt in" to request more information.

I can tell you that my grandmother would NEVER "opt in" to ANY service because she feels it intrudes her space just so she can receive your information, which comes across as "salesy".

However my grandmother would LOVE for you to ask her permission to send her more information.

She may even be willing to exchange allowing you to enter her private space in exchange for receiving more of your valuable information.

Its all in the positioning of your offer and the words you select. (I told you this is a VERY deep rabbit hole).

Answer these questions and answer them again.

Is their response to my offer allowing me to follow up with more helpful information?

Are they giving me their permission to continue sending more valuable information?

Is my offer viewed a SPAM or real help to their problem?

Does each contact with them give them highly valuable, useful and relevant information?

Having a lead capture, or several lead capture mechanisms in your business is one of the easiest ways for ANY operating company to increase revenue.

When someone raises their hand to tell you they are interested in more information regarding your services, you are 10x more likely to do business with them than you are to generate a new lead in your business and close the sale with the new lead.

Use their permission cautiously NOT to move to quickly into the sale, but to continue educating them.

I am beginning to see a handful of marketers successfully offering people a "no optin required" offer where they are strategically giving HIGHLY valuable info. They offer this as a simple download on a website, however once the clients gets totally engaged, right around the middle of the book or video, they require them to opt in for the remaining info.

Although sneaky, humanity has forced marketers to always raise the bar since ***human behavior always wants change without commitment.***

Some of the best ways to capture info are email, Facebook profiles, phone numbers and social links.

What Is My Multi Step Follow Up, Educational Process For Turning Hand Raisers Into Paying Clients?

Fortunes are made in the follow up.

In my discussion with Josh and Brandon over at BiggerPockets, I gave the majority of my success to my relentless follow up.

Before this process I am going through with you existed in my business, I WAS THE FOLLOW UP PROCESS.

I had no systems in place to keep these target markets informed. I was the system. I had a hard time accepting that people received value from anything else other than a human.

I couldn't accept the fact that I might lose someone to a email or possibly to another investor. I thought I WAS THE VALUE.

I lost many people to badgering and not being valuable.

Nowadays I don't mind if they seek elsewhere. I know my info is valuable so IF they are serious and want a true result, I know I am one of few options who can deliver.

Im ok if they go to someone else as I know they will likely come back. Ive finally accepted that I can only capture and add value to those who truly want a result. Those who don't, I never stood a chance of converting anyway.

Some will. Some won't. So what. Someone's waiting.

The fact of the matter remains that only around 15% of people who seek something out or request more information are ready to buy right now. This is general but pretty much applies across the industry.

Can you image 100 people walking into Apple and only (as much as) 15% are ready to buy and everyone else just leaving and heading to Dell?

Apple knows exactly how to create an engaging experience for customers to stay with them. Its why at no time do you ever feel you are being "sold" on an Apple product.

Consider these questions for your follow up process.

How am I continually, systematically and personally connecting with them to continue helping them with their problem?

Is this viewed as non invasive, highly valuable information?

Is it in the format that best suits their interest?

What are my calls to action that allow them to take a simple step to further relief and an incredible customer experience?

On average, only 7-15% of customers who raise their hands, initially do business within the first few days of inquiring.

The remaining 85-93% WILL eventually do business...with somebody.

After all, they are looking for a *Specific Result* for their golf swing right?

Heres a BIG secret....the customer does not care about you or whether YOU get their business. The customer ONLY cares about the result he will receive from whomever he decides to do business with.

In my opinion, following up through FB messenger is much better than follow up via email. Even with the same message, the dynamic of how they are presented AND consumed allow Facebook to dominate this process.

Facebook messages have the same open rate as a text message as to where email has created a stigma of tasks that have to be managed and therefore rarely make it to the "must read" list.

Some times phone follow up IS the best way to stay in touch. Depending on your target market, you wont know until you go through this unique process, track the data and adjust accordingly.

Make it easy for customers to raise their hand, and then offer continuous, non invasive, highly valuable information that gives them the result they were initially looking for.

Take notice to WHAT makes you respond and how people KEEP your attention. It's not an easy task and if you wouldn't fall for it, don't expect your market to either.

P.S. Don't think you will master this over night...or in 10 years. Companies like Zimmerman Advertising stop at NOTHING to understand the buying patterns and mental psychology that makes customers pull out their credit card.

It is a science...mixed with perfect skill and excellent timing.

Learn to operate by these standards and your business will soar in ANY market, any economy, any country and regardless of competition.

#differentiateordie

What To Do Next!!!

Now that you have read this report, its time to take action. Use the checklist to compare and prepare your old marketing campaign to your next coming campaign.

Below you will find the actual checklist of items you must go through in order to begin effective marketing.

Don't get overwhelmed and think you will master these on your first campaign.

ALL MARKETING IS A TEST.

Start with what is manageable and scale up with each new campaign.

If you need to still identify where it is that you make your money, use the KPI worksheets to help you determine your most profitable deals for the past 365 days. Those can be found in the back of this book as well as downloaded online.

By answering the questions in this book honestly and thoroughly, you will have removed much of the guess work and thought process your ideal client is having.

These answers allow you to create a marketing process, compelling offers and calls to action that allow you to systematically generate new leads into your business and then allow your follow up, educational process to perpetually turn those leads into deals and/or paying customers.

Do This Exercise For Each of Your Target Market Campaigns

1. Have I Selected A Single Target Market?
- Who Do I BEST Serve In My Industry?
- Where Do I Earn 80%+ of My Income?
- What Niche Do I Specialize In?
- Focus on The Largest Check In This Specific Target Market

2. What Is My Form Of Media To Capture Their Attention?
- Where Is My Target Market Looking For Answers?
- What Questions Are They Asking To Discover These Answers?
- How Are They Seeking Results For Their Questions?
- Why Would They Act Or Not Act?
- Design Your Media Around The Answers to These Questions

3. What Is My Compelling, Mafia Style Offer?
- What Would Make My Perfect Client Raise Their Hand?
- What Is Their Perfect Result I Can Deliver Them?
- What Can I Offer Them As An Incentive To Respond?
- How Do I Present This Offer To Look Like Valuable Info Instead of An Ad?

4. Does My Marketing Make It Easy To Respond?
- How Will My Prospect Most Willingly Respond To My Ability To Help?
- How Can I Get Them To Take Action Now?
- What Possible Barriers Would Prevent Them From Taking Action?
- Can I Deliver An Immediate Solution Upon Their First Contact With Me?

5. How Am I Capturing Their Info To Continue Giving Them Valuable Information?
- Is Their Response To My Offer Allowing Me To Follow Up With More Helpful Information?

TheRealErikStark.com/SellerMarketing

- Is It Viewed As SPAM Or Real Help To Their Problem?
- Does Each Contact With Them Give Them Highly Valuable, Useful and Relevant Information?

6. What Is My Multi Step Follow Up, Educational Process For Turning Hand Raisers Into Paying Clients?

- How Am I Continually, Systematically and Personally Connecting With Them To Continue Helping Them With Their Problem?
- Is This Viewed As Non Invasive, Highly Valuable Information?
- Is It In The Format That Best Suits Their Interest?
- What Are My Calls To Action That Allow Them To Take A Simple Step To Further Relief and An Incredible Customer Experience?

Did you enjoy this free report? This is just one of the many strategies we discuss in our annual mastermind and with our one on one coaching students.

If you would like more information about how to increase your lead flow, improve your lead conversion, learn how to maximize your deals, make big money with small lists and simply do bigger deals with less headache and live the real estate investor lifestyle, here are five simple ways to get the laser focus of investors who have walked the path before you and can show you a few ideas that worked well for us and are guaranteed to give you great results.

Get Featured On Our Podcast - We are delighted to have special guests on our podcasts that are willing to share whats working for them and this call also doubles as a "business detox session" where we will give you several ideas and strategies that you can implement in your business immediately. Simply go to www.TheRealErikStark.com/Podcast

Al La Carte - Do you have a pretty good handle on your real estate business yet could use some occasional guidance, motivation or negotiation strategies? We offer the opportunity for one hour focused time blocks to discuss your current situation or opportunity. These calls are based on your specific needs and can be used at your discretion. Call requests are usually set up within 48 hours. Email request can be sent to Erik@TheRealErikStark.com

Annual Mastermind - Are you looking to be a part of a small group of investors that have figured out whats really working? We work with a small group of investors throughout the year. Typically less than 15 at a time simply because we still run a full time business and there is a lot of work that goes into creating content and action plans for those who want to get to the next level. This is not open for new investors. You must be operating a minimum six figure annual business. Register for our next mastermind right here. (www.SelfManagingFreedom.com)

One on One - There is no one size fits all glove that will teach you real estate. Truth is no coach can help anyone if they don't know where they need the help. Work with US (not some assigned coach) to hone your skills, determine target markets, create marketing pieces that stick, learn how to convert sellers, increase property values, understand zoning, how to assign for larger paydays (our smallest assignment in the last 3 years was $25,000, up to $85,000). We can take you from where you are to where you want to go. You must be operating a minimum six figure annual business. Six month commitment (although most stick with us for a few years leaving few openings to join) Apply For One on One Monthly Education Right Here.

For more case studies forms, downloads, reports, mind maps and free resources you can use right now to make money in your business just visit www.TheRealErikStark.com and check out the Free Stuff section.

For customized consulting and one on one business strategy guidance, email Erik at Erik@TheRealErikStark.com.

Thank you for making the time to read this report.

Don't forget to listen to the Audio podcast that goes along with this free marketing report at

www.RealEstateWhileYouDrive.com/DirectMailEp1

You can also claim your digital copy of this report with resources and live links https://TheRealErikStark.com/sellermarketing

I believe in you.

Sincerely,

Erik Stark

P.S. No system works if you don't.

Here are a few simple ways to work with us and get faster results in your business.

Ala Carte Professional Services

50 Minute Business Detox Session

- Eliminate Bottlenecks In Your Business **(Turn Bottlenecks Into Breakthroughs)**
- Discover Hidden Opportunities In Your Current Model **(Implement Those Opportunities)**
- How to Increase Profits **(Position Yourself To Receive Higher Paydays)**
- Outsource Undesirable Sources of Income **(Focus On Biggest Checks, Outsource The Rest)**
- How To Implement Magnetic Marketing Into Your Business **(Surely Your Competitors Are NOT Currently Doing This)**
- Get Clear On Where You Generate Your Greatest Sources of Revenue **(Know Your KPIs, Duplicate The Process and Design Unique Experience Around These)**
- Recorded Call For Future Listening **(You're Sure To Catch Something You Missed The First Time)**
- This Also Includes 30 Minutes of Intake/Discover/Review of Your Business **(Anyone Who Can Provide Answers Without Knowing Your TRUE Problems Is Committing Malpractice)**

My Guarantee: If You Feel That The Call Is Not Worth Your Money In The First 20 Minutes, I Will Refund Your Money In Full And You Get To Keep Everything Up To That Point.

Investment In Yourself - $297

Apprentice for a Day (Spend a Day In Our Market)

- Witness The Daily Practices That Are Crucial For Successful Real Estate Investors **(3 Items Every Successful Investor Is Looking for Everyday)**
- Learn The Art of Negotiation **(How To Ask A Few Questions And Learn Everything You Need To Perform At Your Best)**
- How Successful Investors Position Themselves **(In Every Conversation, Even Those Not Business Related)**
- Receive Hands On Knowledge On Real Live Deals We Are Working On
- Learn How To Handle Yourself When The Unexpected Happens **(Its Not How You Act, Its How You RE Act)**

*This is a HANDS ON Experience and You WILL be Placed Outside Your Comfort Zone (Live Calls, Live Meetings, Real Negotiations, Direct Questions of Proposition)

My Guarantee: If You Feel That You Are Not Receiving Your Moneys Worth By Mid Day Noon, I Will Refund Your Money And Everything You Have Received Up To That Point Is Yours To Keep.

Investment In Yourself - $2500

A Day In Your Market (Or Office)

- See Your Market Through The Lens of A High Level Real Estate Investor
- Discover Unforeseen Paydays You May Drive Past Every Day
- Why Ground Level Investing Is CRUCIAL In ANY Market **(Learn These Principles And You'll Adapt In ANY MARKET Condition or Location)**
- Challenge Your Thinking To Operate BIGGER and Learn The Language of Sophisticated Real Estate Investors
- This Includes Making Live Calls, Meeting People Face to Face And Stirring Up Activity That Very Well May Result In A Instant Payday

*This is a HANDS ON Experience and You WILL be Placed Outside Your Comfort Zone (Live Calls, Live Meetings, Real Negotiations, Direct Questions of Proposition)

My Guarantee: If You Feel That You Are Not Receiving Your Moneys Worth By Mid Day Noon, I Will Refund Your Money And Everything You Have Received Up To That Point Is Yours To Keep.

Investment In Yourself - $3000

Two Day Mastermind

- Engage With High Level, Like Minded Entrepreneurs in A World Class Environment
- Dig Deep Into Whats Working In Real Estate RIGHT NOW (Marketing, Deal Structuring, Negotiation)
- Learn How To Position Yourself As The Expert Buyer and Increase Your Paydays
- Discover The New Economy Way To Market Your Services That Your Competition Isn't Using
- Why Knowing Your Entrepreneurial Identity is The Single Most Important Principle That Determines Your Success - Or Accelerates Your Failure

TheRealErikStark.com/SellerMarketing

- Hot Seat Session With Big Three Ideas for Your Business and The Strategies/Team to Implement Them in The Next 14 Days
- Leave With A CLEAR Strategy On How To Reposition Yourself

Apply Here (www.SelfManagingFreedom.com)

Create Your Own Unique Marketing Message

- Break Down Your Companies Kpi's
- Define Your Target Markets Most Profitable Opportunities
- Create A Unique Marketing Message To Capture More Market Share
- Develop Your Unique Process Of How You Take People Through Your Unique Experience
- Implement Calls To Action For Clients To Take You Up On Your Offer
- Set Up Follow Up Processes For Providing Value To Clients
- Build Out Process Map For Your Unique Process

My Guarantee Is That I Will Help You Discover Your Most Profitable Opportunities, Develop Unique Processes To Support These Opportunities, Create Your Unique Message, Build Out Your Customer Avatar, Put Systems That Identify Your Markets Most Probable Clients And Create Assets That Allow You To Build Rapport Through Follow Ups With Your Unique Market.

Investment In Yourself: Please contact me for details as we offer Done For Your Services as well as simple consulting to help you define. Mastermind members are also available to use our digital team to help with this process.

Email our office at erik@TheRealErikStark.com and we will set up a brief call to discuss how to get you from where you are to where you want to be in the shortest time with the least amount of hassle.

KPI Worksheet

How many deals did you do in the last 365 days?_____

What are the source of each of those deals? (Realtor, FSBO, Probate, Short Sale, Etc)

What is the profit of each deal?

How would you rate that deal on a scale of 1-10?

Deal 1 Source_____ Profit $_____ Rating _____

Deal 2 Source_____ Profit $_____ Rating _____

Deal 3 Source_____ Profit $_____ Rating _____

Deal 4 Source_____ Profit $_____ Rating _____

Deal 5 Source_____ Profit $_____ Rating _____

Deal 6 Source_____ Profit $_____ Rating _____

Deal 7 Source_____ Profit $_____ Rating _____

Deal 8 Source_____ Profit $_____ Rating _____

Deal 9 Source_____ Profit $_____ Rating _____

Deal 10 Source_____ Profit $_____ Rating _____

Deal 11 Source_____ Profit $_____ Rating _____

Deal 12 Source_____ Profit $_____ Rating _____

Deal 13 Source_____ Profit $_____ Rating _____

Deal 14 Source_____ Profit $_____ Rating _____

Deal 15 Source_____ Profit $_____ Rating _____

TheRealErikStark.com/SellerMarketing

Deal 16 Source_____ Profit $_____ Rating _____

Deal 17 Source_____ Profit $_____ Rating _____

Deal 18 Source_____ Profit $_____ Rating _____

Deal 19 Source_____ Profit $_____ Rating _____

Deal 20 Source_____ Profit $_____ Rating _____

Deal 21 Source_____ Profit $_____ Rating _____

Deal 22 Source_____ Profit $_____ Rating _____

Deal 23 Source_____ Profit $_____ Rating _____

Deal 24 Source_____ Profit $_____ Rating _____

Deal 25 Source_____ Profit $_____ Rating_____

Deal 26 Source_____ Profit $_____ Rating _____

Deal 27 Source_____ Profit $_____ Rating _____

Deal 28 Source_____ Profit $_____ Rating _____

Deal 29 Source_____ Profit $_____ Rating _____

Deal 30 Source_____ Profit $_____ Rating _____

Deal 31 Source_____ Profit $_____ Rating _____

Deal 32 Source_____ Profit $_____ Rating _____

Deal 33 Source_____ Profit $_____ Rating _____

Deal 34 Source_____ Profit $_____ Rating _____

Deal 35 Source_____ Profit $_____ Rating _____

Deal 36 Source_____ Profit $_____ Rating _____

Deal 37 Source_____ Profit $_____ Rating _____

Deal 38 Source_____ Profit $_____ Rating _____

TheRealErikStark.com/SellerMarketing

Deal 39 Source_____ Profit $_____ Rating _____

Deal 40 Source_____ Profit $_____ Rating _____

What are the top 3 sources for all of your deals?

_____   _____   _____

What is the total profit of each of these deal sources?

_____   _____   _____

What is the average profit of each of these deal sources?

_____   _____   _____

What is the overall rating of each deal vs the total amount?

_____   _____   _____

ERIK STARK

Believer : Husband : Dad
Go Giver : Real Estate Buyer : Marketing Guy
Consultant : Servant

CONTACT/SOCIAL

ERIK@THEREALERIKSTARK.COM

WWW.THEREALERIKSTARK.COM

TWITTER: @THEERIKSTARK

FACEBOOK.COM/THEERIKSTARK

INSTAGRAM: @THEERIKSTARK

INSTAGRAM: @REALESTATEHACKS

LINKED IN: THEERIKSTARK

 **FREE BOOK: Discover What 29 of The Nations Top Investors Would Do If They Had To Start Over From Nothing!!!** https://goo.gl/w7ZXBW

 FREE REPORT: **Learn The Secret to Seller Negotiating Most Investors Will Never Know About and Your Competition Hopes You Never Discover!!!** https://goo.gl/YDccpn

 **Learn How To Buy Your First Real Estate Property (And Your Next 100). The Uncommon Approach To Finding Hidden, Competition FreeProperties In Any Market!** EriksFreeBook.com

 FREE REPORT: **Learn The Secret to Seller Marketing Most Investors Will Never Know About and Your Competition Hopes You Never Discover!!!** https://goo.gl/aF27wE

ABOUT ERIK STARK

Erik Stark is a believer in Christ, uber cool dad, dedicated husband of 15+ years and real estate entrepreneur.
He's purchased hundreds of properties, raised millions in private capital, created masterful marketing pieces for the industry, shared the stage and coached with top real estate and personal development educators, helped thousands of people improve their lives and continues to pour his life into people, friendships, disciplines, breakthrough and growth.

HERE ARE SOME OF ERIKS REMARKABLE ACHIEVEMENTS

- Assigned his first deal at age 24
- Purchased over 400+ properties since including single and multi family, apartments, commercial, vacant land and developments
- Raised millions of dollars in private capital for acquisitions
- Studied and created some of the industries greatest marketing pieces
- Helped dozens of investors do their first deal
- Invested over $150,000 into his education
- Has spent well over 10,000 hours in the field of real estate acquisition, finance, negotiation, management and development
- Coached for several top real estate educators
- Created unique operating platforms the deliver consistent, dependable results Featured as the "underground expert" in numerous online communities
- Turned his house flipping hobby into a brick and mortar company with his business partner Steven Mills by age 26
- Acquired $1,000,000 in real estate by age 3
- Runs a local young professional men's ministry near his home in South Florida
- Active member of the community supporting Habitat for Humanity, Sheridan House Ministry and Homeless Voice
- Committed man of 15+ years to his lovely wife who supports his sacrifice, breakthroughs, appreciation for great living and constant and never ending improvement of life.

HERE ARE SOME OF ERIKS UNIQUE TALENTS AND ABILITIES

- Marketing and Innovation
- Deal Structuring
- Assigning Large Deals
- Making Big Money from Small Mailing Lists
- Owner Financing
- Street Level Investing
- Business Development (KPI's)
- Unique Process Creation (Systems)
- Book Making (SmartSell Property Selling System)
- Going Deep Not Wide
- Land Deals
- Probate Investing
- Human Behaviors
- Target Marketing
- Realtor Leads Systems
- Using Real Estate To Achieve Financial Independence To Build The Life You Truly Want To Live

WORK A STRATEGY - STOP CHASING OPPORTUNITY

TheRealErikStark.com/SellerMarketing